Cross-Stitch
Treasures
for
Children™

by Joan Elliott

Introduction

Welcome to a treasury of cross-stitch designs that captures the precious and magical world that children live in. The soft touch of their cheek as we kiss them good night, the singsong lilt of their laughter, their questions and curiosity about everything around them—all these tender and wonderful moments have inspired the designs in this book.

The birth of a baby is such a joy. A little one often seems heaven-sent, a wonderful gift for a family to love and cherish. A personalized birth sampler complete with Baby's favorite cuddly critters is the perfect way to celebrate this special time. As Baby grows, a colorfully illustrated ABC is just the thing to help with learning. Stitch it up as a picture, or why not make a cozy afghan with one of the playful letters stitched in each square?

Nothing brings childhood to mind quite like Mother Goose and her nursery rhymes. What fun to have these charming characters marching along in their merry parade! You'll find a fairy and dragon to encourage little girls and little boys to make a wish and follow their dreams. Imagination and wonder fill a child's room with creativity. Stitch up a special nameplate for them to hang proudly on their wall. Finally, take your pick from a collection of small motifs for stitching cards, tiny cushions, gift bags—whatever may strike your fancy.

You'll find the designs in this book quite straightforward. The palette is bright and cheerful, reflecting the fun in a child's life. If you don't care for stitching French knots, why not try substituting petite glass beads instead? They will add the needed dimension and are the perfect alternative. There are also ideas for different ways the designs can be used and suggestions for alternative fabrics. Add a touch of your own creativity with your choices and, most of all, enjoy!

Nursery Rhyme Parade,
page 4

Cuddly Friends Birth Announcement,
page 12

Childhood ABCs,
page 20

Just for Girls,
page 28

Meet the Designer

Joan Elliott has been creating needlework designs for close to 40 years. After graduating with a degree in fine arts, Joan's passion for color and interest in fiber art found an easy home in the needlework world. With countless cross-stitch designs to her credit and more than 12 books of designs she has published over the years, her distinctive style is easily recognized and appreciated by cross-stitch fans around the world.

Joan's designs appear regularly in the major cross-stitch magazines in both the United States and the United Kingdom, and kits and chart packs of her designs are sold worldwide. Finding the enthusiasm of cross stitchers inspiring, she loves keeping in touch with her fans around the world through both her blog and Facebook page.

Joan has always enjoyed working on children's themes for cross stitch and in this, her second book of all new designs done exclusively for Annie's, she returns to explore the fun, joy and imagination that makes childhood such a magical time.

Joan divides her time between New York City and the peaceful countryside of Vermont where she joyfully indulges her passion for gardening and is forever inspired by the beauty of the nature that surrounds her. She and her husband feel truly blessed to share all the joys of both city and country life.

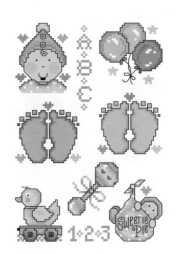

Nursery Rhyme Parade

Mother Goose leads the way in this celebration of a childhood favorite.
Jack and Jill, The Cat and The Fiddle, Humpty Dumpty, Mary and her little
lamb, and all your favorite characters invite you to join in. See how many of
these classic nursery rhymes you can recall.

Materials

· 28-count evenweave:
    27 x 12 inches
· DMC floss as indicated in color key

Project Note

This design works well on 28-count evenweave
working over 2 threads. For some variation, try
using one of the pretty hand-dyed fabrics avail-
able. For example, a light blue hand-dyed fabric
will give the lovely effect of clouds and sky. This
will also stitch up nicely as a long bolster cushion, maybe edged with some fun pompoms.

Skill Level

Easy

Stitch Count

323 wide x 112 high

Approximate Design Size

· 11-count 30" x 10⅛"
· 14-count 23" x 8"
· 16-count 20⅞" x 7"
· 18-count 18" x 6¼"
· 25-count 13" x 4½"
· 28-count over 2 threads 23" x 8"
· 32-count over 2 threads 20⅞" x 7"

Instructions

Center and stitch design on 28-count evenweave,
working over 2 threads and using 2 strands floss
for full, half and quarter Cross-Stitch; 1 strand
floss for Backstitch; and 2 strands or 1 strand
floss, wrapped once, for French Knot.

FULL, HALF & QUARTER CROSS-STITCH (2X)

ANCHOR		DMC	COLORS
2	o	1	White
110	◢	208	Very dark lavender
109	♣	209	Dark lavender
108	☆	210	Medium lavender
403	■	310	Black
979	8	312	Very dark baby blue
400	◪	317	Pewter gray
399	⌘	318	Light steel gray
9046	♥	321	Red
977	▶	334	Medium baby blue
13	◆◆	349	Dark coral
10	+	351	Coral
398	⇨	415	Pearl gray
891	≈	676	Light old gold
890	❁	729	Medium old gold
303	★	742	Light tangerine
302	∞	743	Medium yellow
301	H	744	Pale yellow
944	☻	869	Very dark hazelnut brown
360	✖	898	Very dark coffee brown
257	♣	905	Dark parrot green
256	∾	906	Medium parrot green
255	≪	907	Light parrot green
881	♡	945	Tawny
1010	Z	951	Light tawny
75	✿	962	Medium dusty rose
73	V	963	Ultra very light dusty rose
25	◑	3716	Very light dusty rose
140	✂	3755	Baby blue
901	▲	3829	Very dark old gold

BACKSTITCH (1X)

ANCHOR		DMC	COLORS
403	—	310	Black* (outline throughout)
9046	—	321	Red* (cow mouth, eyeglasses)
977	—	334	Medium baby blue* (bee wings)
257	—	905	Dark parrot green* (flourishes on cow hat)

FRENCH KNOT (2X)

ANCHOR		DMC	COLOR
403	●	310	Black*

FRENCH KNOT (1X)

ANCHOR		DMC	COLOR
403	●	310	Black* (eyes of child on shoe, and child carrying candle)

*Duplicate color

Nursery Rhyme Parade

Our book cover displays an alternative version to stitch with Humpty Dumpty leading the parade instead of Mother Goose.

Materials

· 28-count evenweave:
   22 x 12 inches
· DMC floss as indicated in color key

Project Note

Use the full version of the Nursery Rhyme Parade chart and color key with Mother Goose leading the way until you see the red arrow close to Humpty Dumpty's foot on page 9. Use the chart given on this page to complete this shorter version.

Skill Level

Easy

Stitch Count

253 wide x 112 high

Approximate Design Size

· 11-count 23" x 10⅛"
· 14-count 18" x 8"
· 16-count 15⅞" x 7"
· 18-count 14" x 6¼"
· 25-count 10⅛" x 4½"
· 28-count over 2 threads 18" x 8"
· 32-count over 2 threads 15⅞" x 7"

Instructions

Center and stitch design on 28-count evenweave, working over 2 threads and using 2 strands floss for full, half and quarter Cross-Stitch; 1 strand floss for Backstitch; and 2 strands or 1 strand floss, wrapped once, for French Knot.

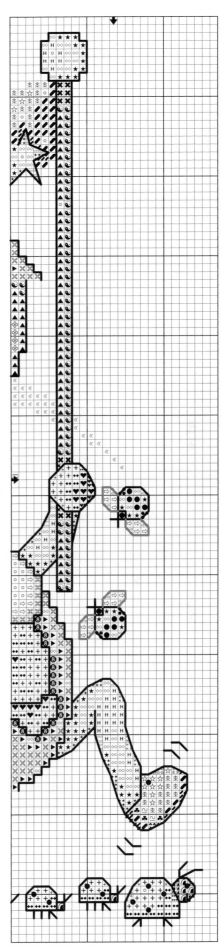

Cuddly Friends Birth Announcement

Cute and cuddly, a delightful birth announcement filled with whimsical teddies, smiling monkeys and happy critters of all sorts sends a happy welcome to your new bundle of joy. With an alphabet for personalization included, a birth sampler is the perfect gift to treasure for a lifetime.

Materials

· 14-count Aida or 28-count evenweave or linen: 14 x 17 inches
· DMC floss as indicated in color key

Project Notes

Try using a very pale blue, yellow, mint green or pink Aida—whichever suits your baby best.

For a finer, more heirloom look, use-28 count evenweave or linen, working over 2 threads.

Skill Level

Easy

Stitch Count

138 wide x 182 high

Approximate Design Size

· 11-count 12½" x 16½"
· 14-count 9⅞" x 13"
· 16-count 8⅝" x 11⅜"
· 18-count 7⅝" x 10⅛"
· 25-count 5½" x 7¼"
· 28-count over 2 threads 9⅞" x 13"
· 32-count over 2 threads 8⅝" x 11⅜"

Instructions

Center and stitch design on fabric, using 2 strands floss for full, half and quarter Cross-Stitch; 1 strand floss for Backstitch; and 2 strands floss, wrapped once, for French Knot.

FULL, HALF & QUARTER CROSS-STITCH (2X)

ANCHOR		DMC	COLORS
2	○	1	White
375	✪	167	Very dark yellow beige
110	✳	208	Very dark lavender
109	⌘	209	Dark lavender
108	a	210	Medium lavender
400	❽	317	Pewter gray
399	秊	318	Light steel gray
977	◢	334	Medium baby blue
11	⋈	350	Medium coral
398	?	415	Pearl gray
310	⚘	434	Light brown
1045	⚖	436	Tan
362	¢	437	Light tan
63	✿	602	Medium cranberry
62	+	603	Cranberry
1094	♡	605	Very light cranberry
303	★	742	Light tangerine
302	⚐	743	Medium yellow
300	□	745	Light pale yellow
1012	✄	754	Light peach
359	←	801	Dark coffee brown
13	♥	817	Very dark coral red
257	♣	905	Dark parrot green
256	⋂	906	Medium parrot green
255	◿	907	Light parrot green
381	◼	938	Ultra dark coffee brown
1011	⑤	948	Very light peach
203	◑	954	Nile green
186	✿	959	Medium sea green
185	✳	964	Light sea green
888	⫘	3045	Dark yellow beige
887	//	3046	Medium yellow beige
852	②	3047	Light yellow beige
140	◕	3755	Baby blue
9159	≋	3841	Pale baby blue

BACKSTITCH (1X)

ANCHOR		DMC	COLORS
977	▬	334	Medium baby blue* (bee wings, clouds)
303	▬	742	Light tangerine* (sun, moon)
13	▬	817	Very dark coral red* (stripe on bird's hatband)
257	▬	905	Dark parrot green* (leaves, flower stems)
381	▬	938	Ultra dark coffee brown* (lettering, motif out...

FRENCH KNOT (2X)

ANCHOR		DMC	COLOR
381	●	938	Ultra dark coffee brown*

*Duplicate color

CHRISTOPHER
JAMES
MATHERSON

25TH NOVEMBER
2012
7 Lbs. 10 oz.

November
12
10 oz.

Cuddly Friends Birth Announcement Alphabet

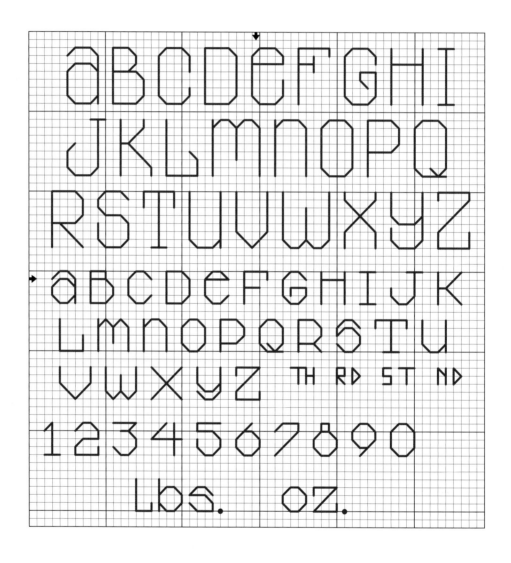

Cuddly Friends Birth Announcement Nameplate

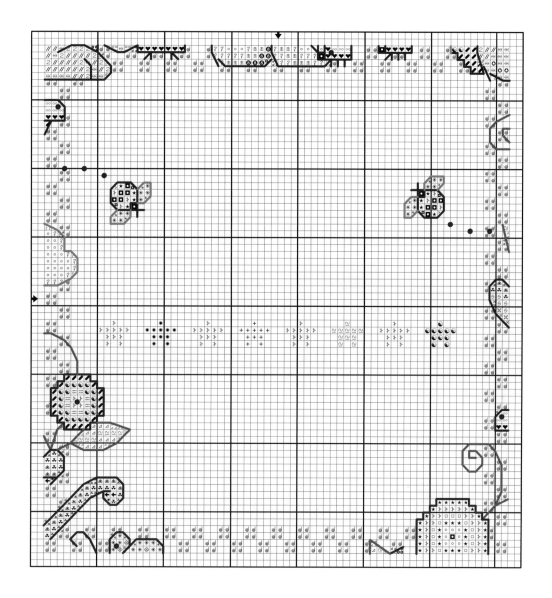

Childhood ABCs

A is for Apple, B is for Bear, C is for Cat—bright and cheerful letters make learning the ABCs fun and easy. What a lovely way to combine your love of cross-stitch and a fun learning experience that is ready to share with your favorite little darling.

Materials

· 14-count Aida or 28-count evenweave
· DMC floss as indicated in color key

Project Notes

This design will work on 14-count Aida, working over 1 thread, or 28-count evenweave, working over 2 threads.

For a larger project, this will also make up into a beautiful afghan, stitching one letter per afghan square. You can also combine letters or initials to make up a nameplate or a cute personalized pillow top.

Skill Level

Easy

Stitch Count

Stitch counts vary

Approximate Design Size

Design sizes vary

Instructions

Center and stitch design on fabric, using 2 strands floss for full, half and quarter Cross-Stitch; 1 strand floss for all Backstitch; and 2 strands floss, wrapped once, for French Knot.

FULL, HALF & QUARTER CROSS-STITCH (2X)

ANCHOR		DMC	COLORS
2	○	1	White
110	◤	208	Very dark lavender
109	✂	209	Dark lavender
399	◆◆	318	Light steel gray
9046	♥	321	Red
398	m	415	Pearl gray
62	✿	603	Cranberry
1094	♡	605	Very light cranberry
46	⌘	666	Bright red
891	∞	676	Light old gold
890	�	729	Medium old gold
304	←	741	Medium tangerine
303	◣	742	Light tangerine
302	⅏	743	Medium yellow
301	=	744	Pale yellow
131	★	798	Dark delft blue
136	◕	799	Medium delft blue
130	≋	809	Delft blue
256	♣	906	Medium parrot green
255	◡	907	Light parrot green
188	✖	943	Medium aquamarine
881	◔	945	Tawny
1010	❯	951	Light tawny
186	◮	959	Medium sea green
185	e	964	Light sea green
382	●	3371	Black brown
1098	+	3801	Very dark melon
901	◢	3829	Very dark old gold

BACKSTITCH (1X)

ANCHOR		DMC	COLORS
9046	—	321	Red*
302	—	743	Medium yellow*
131	—	798	Dark delft blue*
1076	—	991	Dark aquamarine
382	—	3371	Black brown*

FRENCH KNOT (2X)

ANCHOR		DMC	COLORS
46	●	666	Bright red*
382	●	3371	Black brown*

*Duplicate color

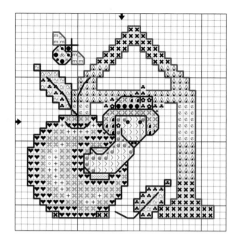

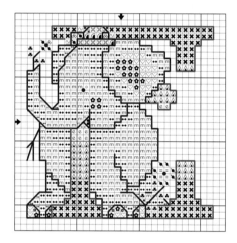

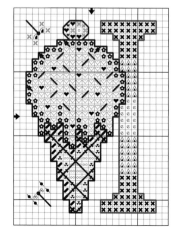

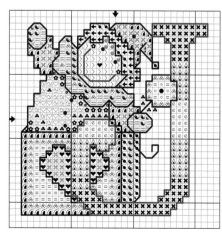

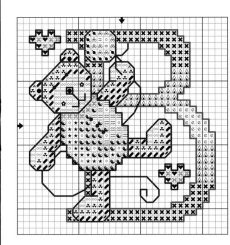 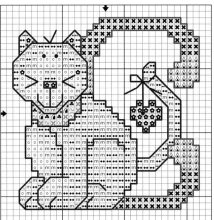 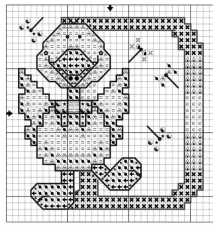

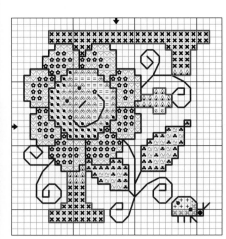 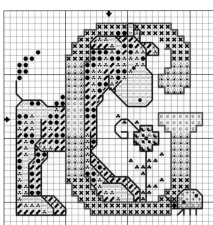 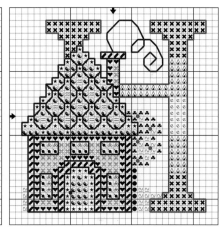

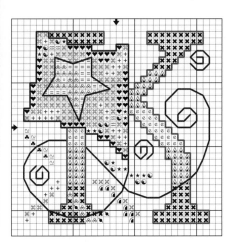  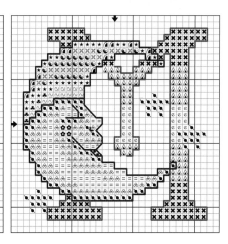

FULL, HALF & QUARTER CROSS-STITCH (2X)

ANCHOR		DMC	COLORS
2	○	1	White
110	◢	208	Very dark lavender
109	✄	209	Dark lavender
399	◆◆	318	Light steel gray
9046	♥	321	Red
398	m	415	Pearl gray
62	✿	603	Cranberry
1094	♡	605	Very light cranberry
46	⌘	666	Bright red
891	∞	676	Light old gold
890	⩣	729	Medium old gold
304	←	741	Medium tangerine
303	◣	742	Light tangerine
302	⚘	743	Medium yellow
301	=	744	Pale yellow
131	★	798	Dark delft blue
136	◕	799	Medium delft blue
130	≋	809	Delft blue
256	♣	906	Medium parrot green
255	∾	907	Light parrot green
188	✖	943	Medium aquamarine
881	◔	945	Tawny
1010	⟩	951	Light tawny
186	◮	959	Medium sea green
185	e	964	Light sea green
382	●	3371	Black brown
1098	+	3801	Very dark melon
901	◢	3829	Very dark old gold

BACKSTITCH (1X)

ANCHOR		DMC	COLORS
9046	━	321	Red*
302	═	743	Medium yellow*
131	━	798	Dark delft blue*
1076	━	991	Dark aquamarine
382	━	3371	Black brown*

FRENCH KNOT (2X)

ANCHOR		DMC	COLORS
46	●	666	Bright red*
382	●	3371	Black brown*

*Duplicate color

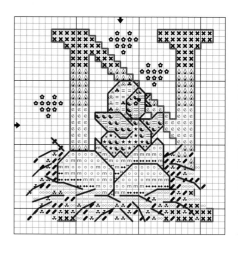

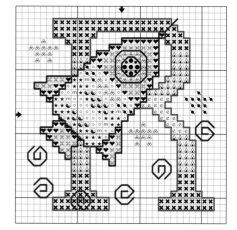

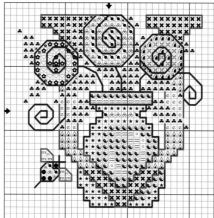

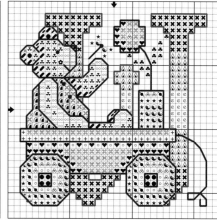

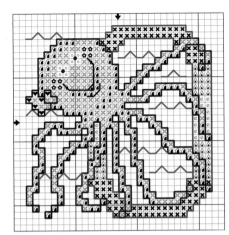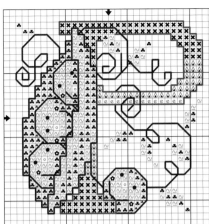

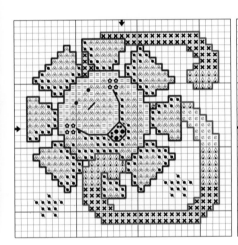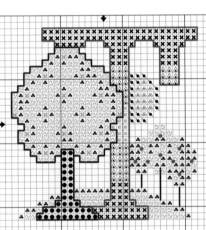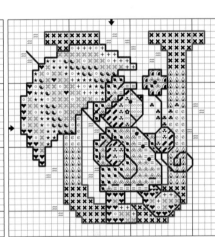

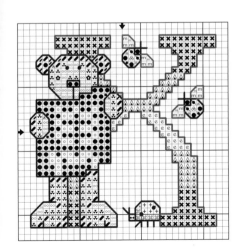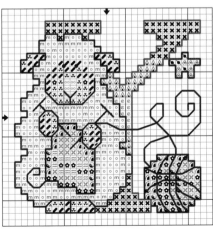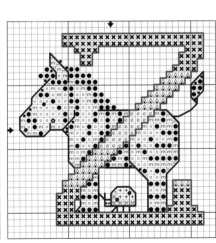

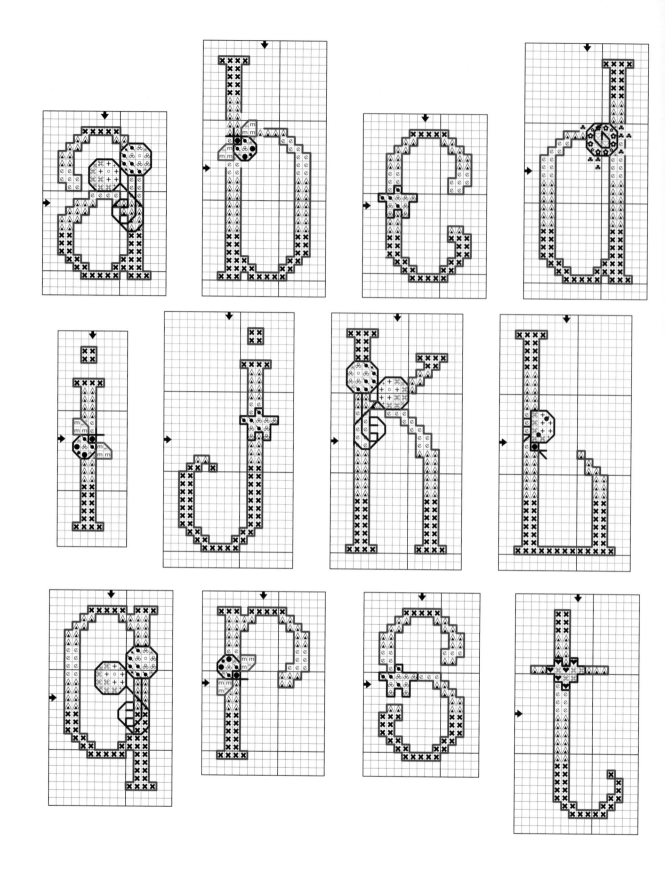

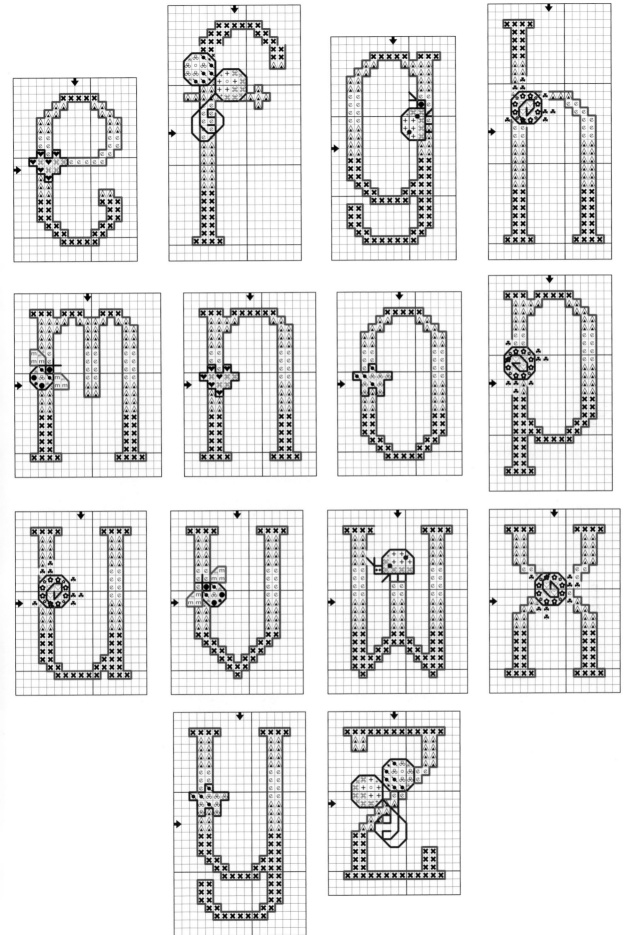

Just for Girls

With stars aglitter and fluttering wings, a pretty fairy queen complete with crown and magic wand delivers a lovely message to a special little girl. With a bit of imagination and a swish of her wand we can all close our eyes and "make a wish."

Materials

- 14-count Aida or 28-count evenweave:
  11 x 13 inches
- DMC floss as indicated in color key
- Kreinik very fine (#4) braid as indicated in color key

Project Notes

We suggest a hand-dyed 14-count Aida, working over 1 thread, or 28-count evenweave, working over 2 threads, for this design. A fabric that suggests a fantasy theme will be very pretty and add to the magical tone of the design.

Besides a framed picture, this design can be made up into a pretty cushion or mounted on top of a keepsake box. An alphabet chart is included on page 44 for personalization.

Skill Level

Easy

Stitch Count

105 wide x 135 high

Approximate Design Size

- 11-count 9½" x 12¼"
- 14-count 7½" x 9⅝"
- 16-count 6½" x 8⅜"
- 18-count 5⅞" x 7½"
- 25-count 4¼" x 5⅜"
- 28-count over 2 threads 7½" x 9⅝"
- 32-count over 2 threads 6½" x 8⅜"

Instructions

Center and stitch design on fabric, using 2 strands floss or 1 strand Kreinik braid for full, half and quarter Cross-Stitch; 1 strand floss or Kreinik braid for all Backstitch; and 2 strands floss, wrapped once, for French Knot.

FULL, HALF & QUARTER CROSS-STITCH (2X)

ANCHOR		DMC	COLORS
2	○	1	White
403	■	310	Black
979	←	312	Very dark baby blue
977	⋘	334	Medium baby blue
398	�V	415	Pearl gray
98	☻	553	Violet
96	e	554	Very light violet
63	♥	602	Medium cranberry
62	✳	603	Cranberry
1094	♡	605	Very light cranberry
890	∕	729	Medium old gold
303	★	742	Light tangerine
302	S	743	Medium yellow
301	∕	744	Pale yellow
944	✖	869	Very dark hazelnut brown
257	♣	905	Dark parrot green
256	℧	906	Medium parrot green
255	□	907	Light parrot green
881	∞	945	Tawny
1010	>	951	Light tawny
203	�	954	Nile green
206	=	955	Light Nile green
140	△	3755	Baby blue
901	⊛	3829	Very dark old gold
100	✚	3837	Ultra dark lavender

FULL, HALF & QUARTER CROSS-STITCH (1X)

KREINIK VERY FINE (#4) BRAID		COLOR
028	m	Citron

BACKSTITCH (1X)

ANCHOR		DMC	COLOR
403	—	310	Black* (lettering, stars, fairy)

KREINIK VERY FINE (#4) BRAID		COLOR
028	—	Citron* (background swirls)

FRENCH KNOT (2X)

ANCHOR		DMC	COLOR
403	●	310	Black* (lettering, wand)

*Duplicate color

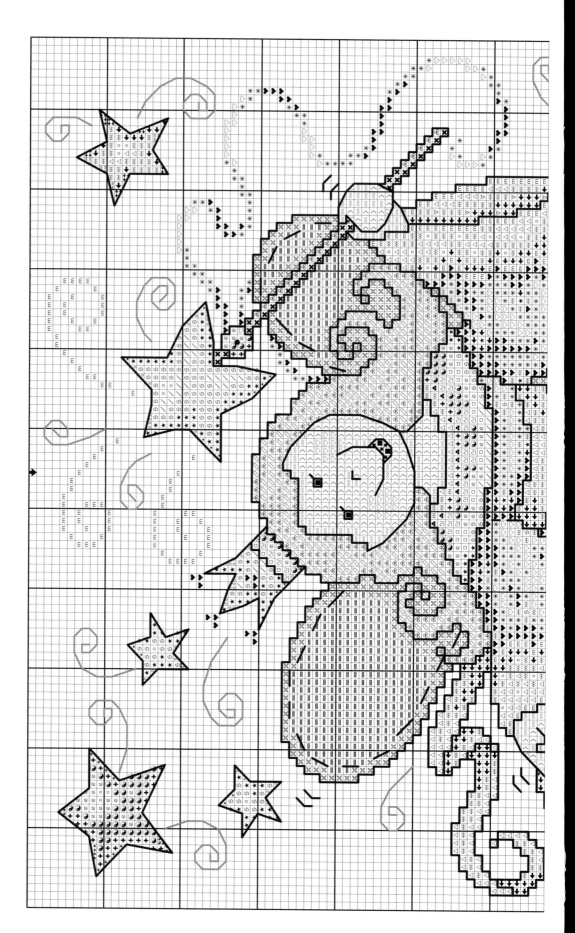

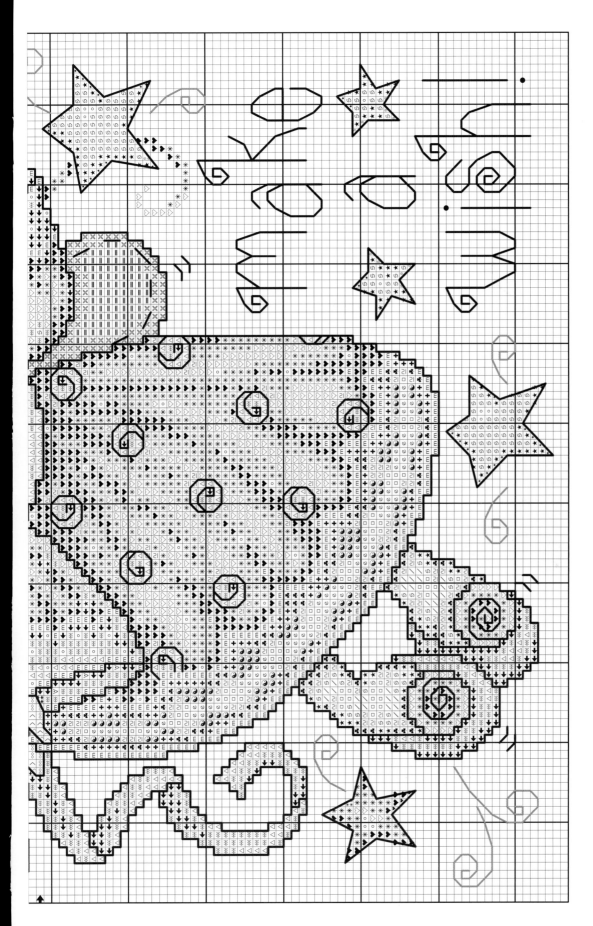

Just for Boys

High in the clouds, a magic dragon appears with his brightly colored jester's hat and shimmering wings with golden swirls. He brings a special message just for your favorite little boy. Loud and clear with brilliant stars all around, "Follow your dreams," he says, for he knows that children are the promise of the future.

Materials
· 14-count Aida or 28-count evenweave:
  11 x 13 inches
· DMC floss as indicated in color key
· Kreinik very fine (#4) braid as indicated in color key

Project Notes
We suggest a hand-dyed 14-count Aida, working over 1 thread, or 28-count evenweave, working over 2 threads for this design. A fabric that suggests a fantasy or cloud theme will be perfect and add to the magic of the design.

Besides a framed picture, this design can be made mounted on top of a keepsake box or a scrapbook cover. An alphabet chart is included on page 44 for personalization.

Skill Level
Easy

Stitch Count
105 wide x 134 high

Approximate Design Size
· 11-count 9½" x 12⅛"
· 14-count 7½" x 9½"
· 16-count 6½" x 8⅜"
· 18-count 5⅞" x 7⅜"
· 25-count 4¼" x 5⅜"
· 28-count over 2 threads 7½" x 9½"
· 32-count over 2 threads 6½" x 8⅜"

Instructions
Center and stitch design on fabric, working over 2 threads. Use 2 strands floss or 1 strand Kreinik braid for full, half and quarter Cross-Stitch; 1 strand floss or Kreinik braid for all Backstitch; and 2 strands floss, wrapped once, for French Knot.

FULL, HALF & QUARTER CROSS-STITCH (2X)

ANCHOR		DMC	COLORS
2	○	1	White
279	▫	166	Medium light moss green
403	■	310	Black
979	◄	312	Very dark baby blue
9046	✿	321	Red
977	⋘	334	Medium baby blue
98	◉	553	Violet
96	℮	554	Very light violet
281	♣	580	Dark moss green
280	∾	581	Moss green
63	♥	602	Medium cranberry
62	+	603	Cranberry
46	✤	666	Bright red
891	∧	676	Light old gold
890	⊘	729	Medium old gold
303	★	742	Light tangerine
302	⑤	743	Medium yellow
301	⁄	744	Pale yellow
944	✖	869	Very dark hazelnut brown
203	✂	954	Nile green
206	⌁	955	Light Nile green
1031	∞	3753	Ultra very light antique blue
140	△	3755	Baby blue
1098	♡	3801	Very dark melon
901	⬡	3829	Very dark old gold
100	✚	3837	Ultra dark lavender

FULL, HALF & QUARTER CROSS-STITCH (1X)

KREINIK VERY FINE (#4) BRAID		COLOR
028	m	Citron

BACKSTITCH (1X)

ANCHOR		DMC	COLORS
403	▬	310	Black* (lettering, stars, dragon)
977	▬	334	Medium baby blue* (clouds)

KREINIK VERY FINE (#4) BRAID		COLOR
028	▬	Citron* (dragon scales, end/swirls of wand, background swirls, swirls on dragon wings)

FRENCH KNOT (2X)

ANCHOR		DMC	COLOR
2	●	1	White* (eye)

*Duplicate color

In My Room

What a charming way to display your child's name! Bold letters and bright illustrations of their favorite things make a sweet way to say, "This is my room."

Dolls, teddies, kittens and ice cream sundaes are for girls. Toy trains, puppy dogs and sailboats are for boys. Even better, use the motifs that suit your child best and mix and match!

Materials (for each)
- 14-count Aida or 28-count evenweave:
    13 x 9 inches
- DMC floss as indicated in color key

Project Notes
We suggest either 14-count Aida, working over 1 thread, or 28-count evenweave, working over 2 threads. Both designs will work well on white or antique white fabric.

Make them up into little wall hangings, as nameplates for their door, or mount them on a shoebox to make a personalized treasure box.

An alphabet chart is included on page 45 for personalization.

Skill Level
Easy

Stitch Count
125 wide x 69 high

Approximate Design Size
- 11-count 11⅜" x 6¼"
- 14-count 9" x 5"
- 16-count 7⅞" x 4⅜"
- 18-count 7" x 3¾"
- 25-count 5" x 2¾"
- 28-count over 2 threads 9" x 5"
- 32-count over 2 threads 7⅞" x 4⅜"

Instructions
Center and stitch design on fabric, using 2 strands floss for full, half and quarter Cross-Stitch; 1 strand floss for all Backstitch; and 2 strands floss, wrapped once, for French Knot.

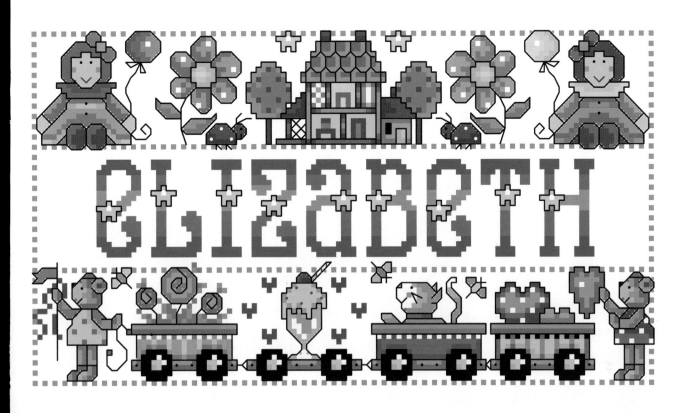

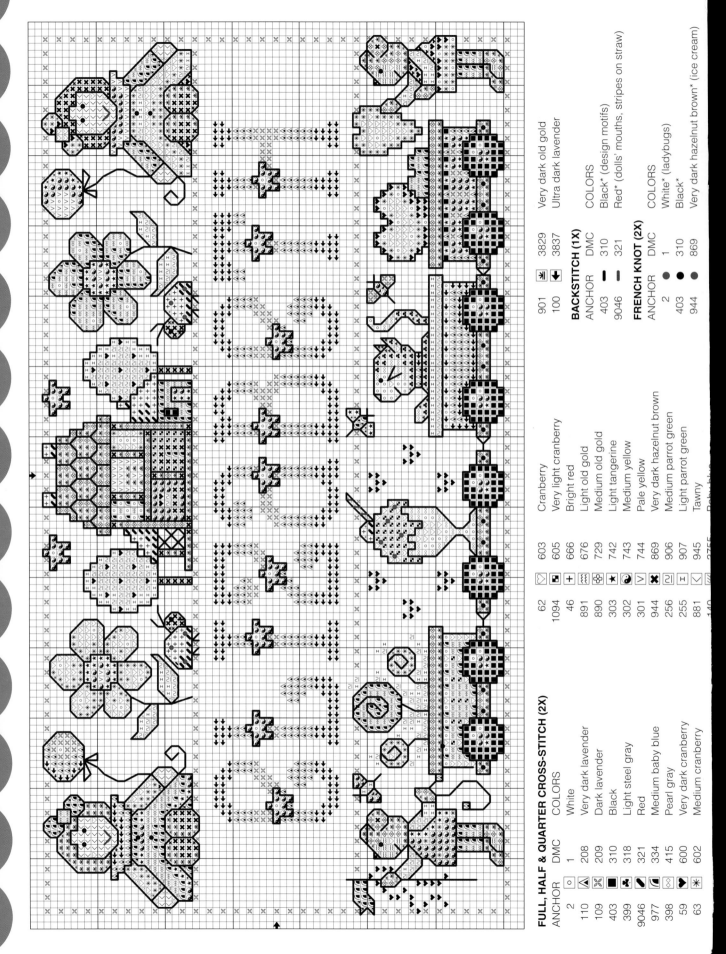

FULL, HALF & QUARTER CROSS-STITCH (2X)

ANCHOR		DMC	COLORS
2	○	1	White
110	◢	208	Very dark lavender
109	✖	209	Dark lavender
403	■	310	Black
399	✦	318	Light steel gray
9046	◣	321	Red
977	◖	334	Medium baby blue
398	◇◇	415	Pearl gray
59	▶	600	Very dark cranberry
63	✳	602	Medium cranberry
62	◇	603	Cranberry
1094	◼	605	Very light cranberry
46	+	666	Bright red
891	▦	676	Light old gold
890	✤	729	Medium old gold
303	★	742	Light tangerine
302	◗	743	Medium yellow
301	∨	744	Pale yellow
944	✖	869	Very dark hazelnut brown
256	2	906	Medium parrot green
255	H	907	Light parrot green
881	∨	945	Tawny
110			Baby blue
901	州	3829	Very dark old gold
100	↓	3837	Ultra dark lavender

BACKSTITCH (1X)

ANCHOR		DMC	COLORS
403	▬	310	Black* (design motifs)
9046	▬	321	Red* (dolls' mouths, stripes on straw)

FRENCH KNOT (2X)

ANCHOR		DMC	COLORS
2	●	1	White* (ladybugs)
403	●	310	Black*
944	●	869	Very dark hazelnut brown* (ice cream)

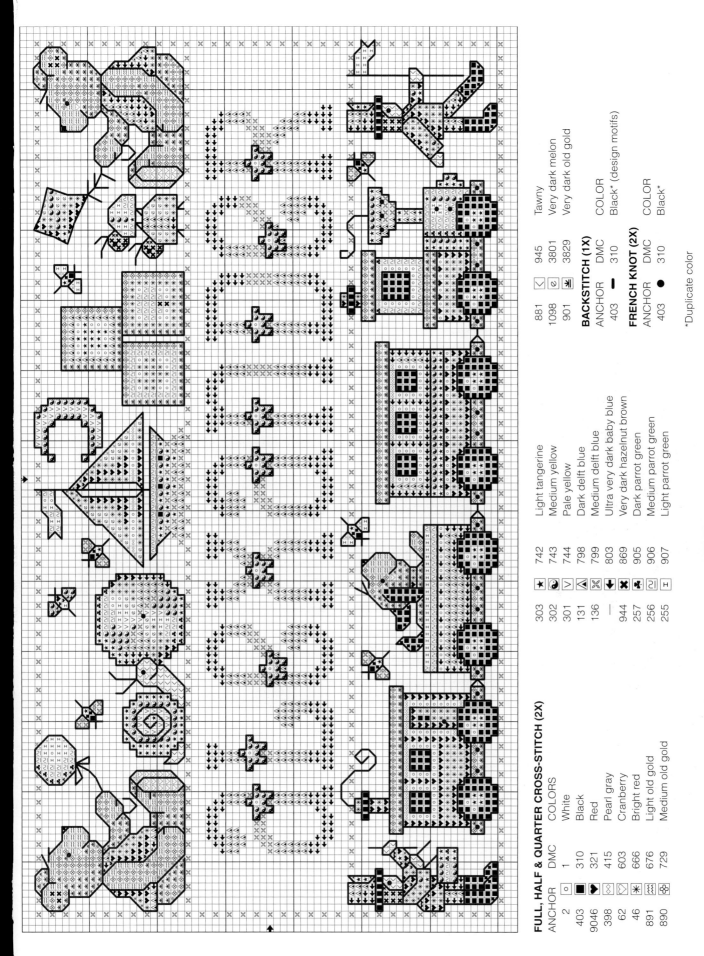

FULL, HALF & QUARTER CROSS-STITCH (2X)

ANCHOR		DMC	COLORS
2		1	White
403		310	Black
9046		321	Red
398		415	Pearl gray
62		603	Cranberry
46		666	Bright red
891		676	Light old gold
890		729	Medium old gold
303		742	Light tangerine
302		743	Medium yellow
301		744	Pale yellow
131		798	Dark delft blue
136		799	Medium delft blue
—		803	Ultra very dark baby blue
944		869	Very dark hazelnut brown
257		905	Dark parrot green
256		906	Medium parrot green
255		907	Light parrot green
881		945	Tawny
1098		3801	Very dark melon
901		3829	Very dark old gold

BACKSTITCH (1X)

ANCHOR	DMC	COLOR
403	310	Black* (design motifs)

FRENCH KNOT (2X)

ANCHOR	DMC	COLOR
403	310	Black*

*Duplicate color

Take Your Pick

Here's a chance to use your creativity to make up your own designs. Use these motifs alone or in combination to create cards, gift bags, trinkets and such—whatever you like. Some of the simpler designs are wonderful for teaching children to cross-stitch too.

Materials
- 14-count Aida
- DMC floss as indicated in color key

Project Note
Try using waste canvas to stitch the motifs on clothing, backpacks, blankets or almost anything. The possibilities are endless using the alphabet charts and motifs together. If teaching cross-stitch to children, choose a large-count Aida so it will be easygoing for them. Stitch along as they learn and share the joy of cross-stitching.

Skill Level
Easy

Stitch Count
Stitch counts vary

Approximate Design Size
Design sizes vary

Instructions
Center and stitch design on 14-count Aida using 2 strands floss for full, half and quarter Cross-Stitch; 1 strand floss for all Backstitch; and 2 strands floss, wrapped once, for French Knot.

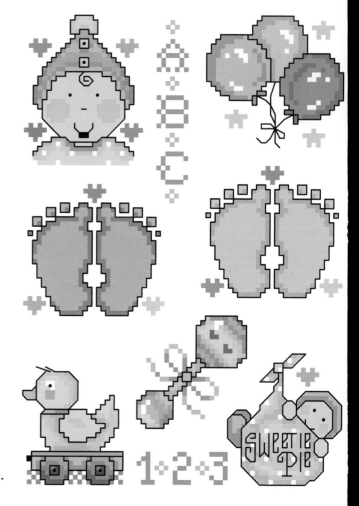

FULL, HALF & QUARTER CROSS-STITCH (2X)

ANCHOR		DMC	COLORS
2	○	1	White
110	←	208	Very dark lavender
109	✳	209	Dark lavender
108	∞	210	Medium lavender
403	■	310	Black
63	▲	602	Medium cranberry
55	✿	604	Light cranberry
1094	♡	605	Very light cranberry
303	★	742	Light tangerine
302	↓	743	Medium yellow
301	▷	744	Pale yellow
131	☀	798	Dark delft blue
136	V	799	Medium delft blue
256	∾	906	Medium parrot green
255	↖	907	Light parrot green
1010	=	951	Light tawny
186	▲	959	Medium sea green
185	≋	964	Light sea green
129	I	3325	Light baby blue

BACKSTITCH (1X)

ANCHOR		DMC	COLOR
403	▬	310	Black*

FRENCH KNOT (2X)

ANCHOR		DMC	COLOR
403	●	310	Black*

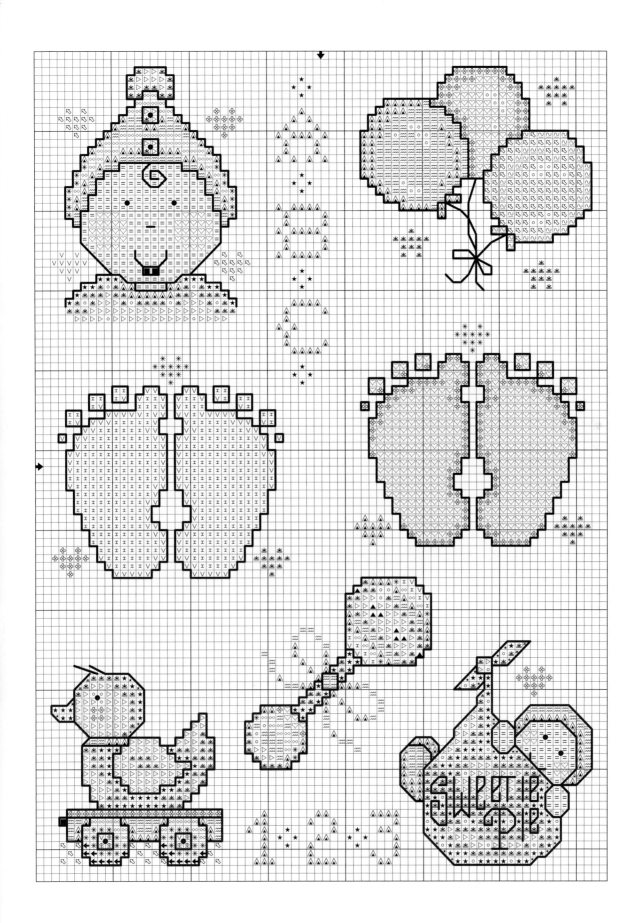

FULL, HALF & QUARTER CROSS-STITCH (2X)

ANCHOR		DMC	COLORS
2	○	1	White
110	←	208	Very dark lavender
109	✳	209	Dark lavender
108	⊗	210	Medium lavender
403	■	310	Black
11	♧	350	Medium coral
398	#	415	Pearl gray
310	◓	434	Light brown
63	▲	602	Medium cranberry
55	♣	604	Light cranberry
1094	♡	605	Very light cranberry
891	╱	676	Light old gold
890	╱	729	Medium old gold
303	★	742	Light tangerine
302	⬇	743	Medium yellow
301	▷	744	Pale yellow
132	✿	797	Royal blue
131	❋	798	Dark delft blue
136	∨	799	Medium delft blue
359	☾	801	Dark coffee brown
13	♥	817	Very dark coral red
257	♣	905	Dark parrot green
256	∿	906	Medium parrot green
255	◹	907	Light parrot green
1010	=	951	Light tawny
1098	+	3801	Very dark melon
901	⚡	3829	Very dark old gold

BACKSTITCH (1X)

ANCHOR		DMC	COLORS
403	—	310	Black*
359	—	801	Dark coffee brown* (stem of large flower)

FRENCH KNOT (2X)

ANCHOR		DMC	COLORS
403	●	310	Black*
359	●	801	Dark coffee brown* (eyes on large flower)

*Duplicate color

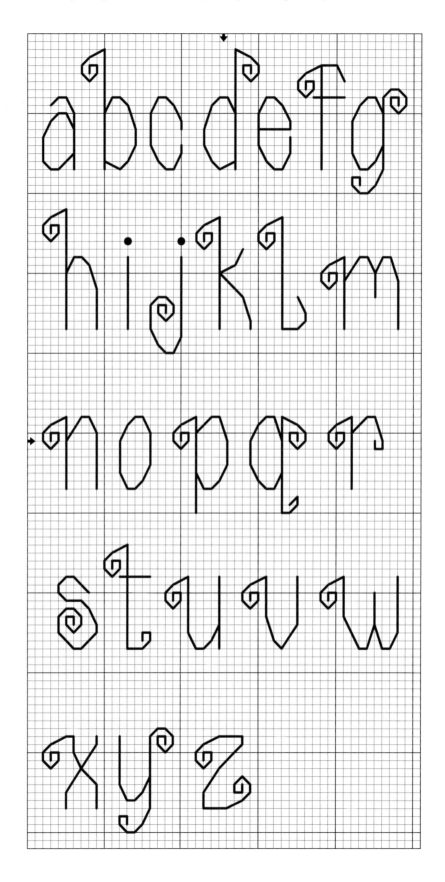

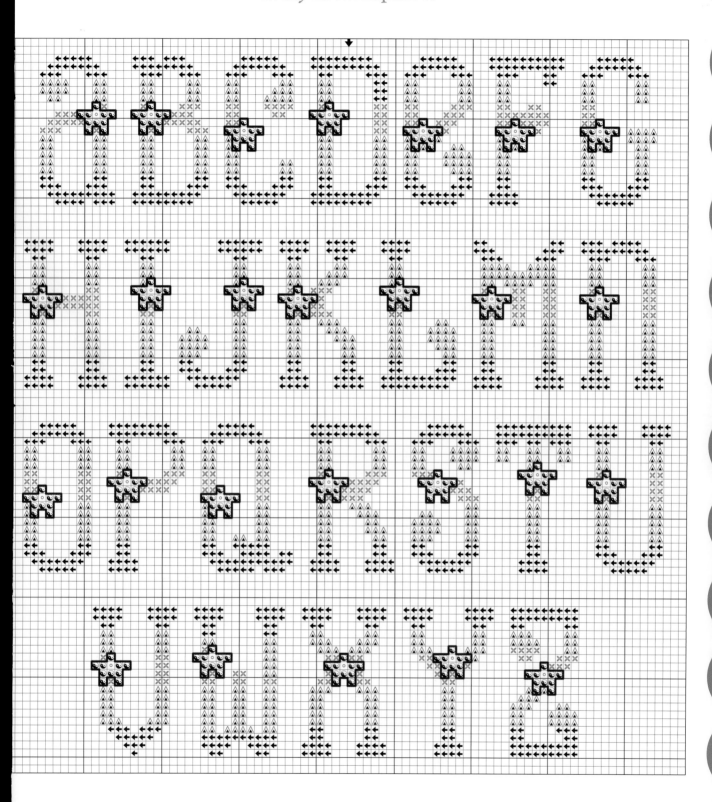

How to Stitch

Working From Charted Designs

A square on a chart corresponds to a space for a Cross-Stitch on the stitching surface. The symbol in a square shows the floss color to be used for the stitch. The width and height for the design stitch-area are given; centers are shown by arrows. Backstitches are shown by straight lines, and French Knots are shown by dots.

Fabrics

In our Materials listings we give Joan Elliott's fabric suggestions that will complement each design. Our front-cover model was worked on a 28-count evenweave fabric that has the same number of horizontal and vertical threads (or blocks of threads) per inch. That number is called the thread count.

The size of the design is determined by the size of the evenweave fabric on which you work. Use the chart below as a guide to determine the finished size of a design on various popular sizes of cross-stitch fabric.

Thread Count	Number of Stitches in Design				
	10	20	30	40	50
11-count	1"	1¾"	2¾"	3⅝"	4½"
14-count	¾"	1⅜"	2⅛"	2⅞"	3⅝"
16-count	⅝"	1¼"	1⅞"	2½"	3⅛"
18-count	½"	1⅛"	1⅝"	2¼"	2¾"
25-count	⅜"	⅞"	1¼"	1⅝"	2"
28-count	⅜"	¾"	1"	1⅜"	1¾"
32-count	¼"	⅝"	⅞"	1¼"	1½"

(measurements are given to the nearest ⅛")

Needles

A blunt-tipped tapestry needle, size 24 or 26, is used for stitching on most 14-count to 28-count fabrics. The higher the needle number, the smaller the needle. The correct-size needle is easy to thread with the amount of floss required, but is not so large that it will distort the holes in the fabric. The following chart indicates the appropriate-size needle for each size of fabric, along with the suggested number of strands of floss to use.

Fabric	Strands of Floss	Tapestry Needle Size
11-count	3	24 or 26
14-count	2	24 or 26
16-count	2	24, 26 or 28
18-count	1 or 2	26 or 28
25-count	1	26 or 28
28-count over two threads	2	26 or 28
32-count over two threads	2	28

Floss

Our front-cover model was stitched using DMC six-strand embroidery floss. Color numbers are given for floss. Both DMC and Anchor color numbers are given for each design. Cut floss into comfortable working lengths; we suggest about 18 inches.

Blending Filament & Metallic Braid

Blending filament is a fine, shiny fiber that can be used alone or combined with floss or other thread. Knotting the blending filament on the needle with a slip knot is recommended for control (Fig. 1).

Fig. 1
Slipknot

Metallic braid is a braided metallic fiber, usually used single-ply. Thread this fiber just as you would any other fiber. Use short lengths, about 15 inches, to keep the fiber from fraying.

Getting Started

To begin in an unstitched area, bring threaded needle from back to front of fabric. Hold an inch of the end against the back, and then hold it in place with your first few stitches. To end threads and begin new ones next to existing stitches, weave through the backs of several stitches.

The Stitches

The number of strands used for Cross-Stitches will be determined by the thread count of the fabric used. Refer to the needles chart to determine the number of strands used for Cross-Stitches. Use one strand for Backstitches.

Cross-Stitch

The Cross-Stitch is formed in two motions. Follow the numbering in Fig. 2 and bring needle up at 1, down at 2, up at 3 and down at 4 to complete the stitch. Work horizontal rows of stitches (Fig. 3) wherever possible. Bring thread up at 1, work half of each stitch across the row, and then complete the stitches on your return.

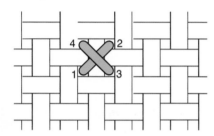

Fig. 2
Cross-Stitch

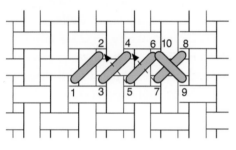

Fig. 3
Cross-Stitch
Horizontal Row

Half Cross-Stitch

The first part of a Cross-Stitch may slant in either direction (Fig. 4).

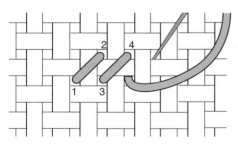

Fig. 4
Half Cross-Stitch

Quarter Cross-Stitch

The Quarter Cross-Stitch is formed in one motion. Follow the numbering in Fig. 5 and bring needle up at 1 and down at 2. The Quarter Cross-Stitch is used to fill in small spaces in the design where there is not enough room for a full stitch.

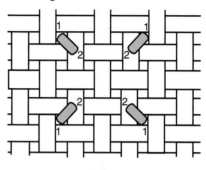

Fig. 5
Quarter Cross-Stitch

Backstitch

Backstitches are worked after Cross-Stitches have been completed. They may slope in any direction and are occasionally worked over more than one square of fabric. Fig. 6 shows the progression of several stitches; bring thread up at odd numbers and down at even numbers. Frequently, you must choose where to end one Backstitch color and begin the next color. Choose the object that should appear closest to you. Backstitch around that shape with the appropriate color, and then Backstitch the areas behind it with adjacent color(s).

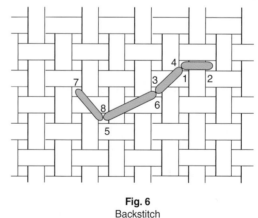

Fig. 6
Backstitch

French Knot

Bring thread up where indicated on chart. Wrap floss once around needle (Fig. 7) and reinsert needle at 2, close to 1, but at least one fabric thread away from it. Hold wrapping thread tightly and pull needle through, letting thread go just as knot is formed. For a larger knot, use more strands of floss.

Fig. 7
French Knot

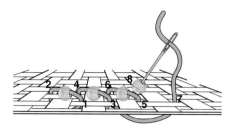

Fig. 8
Bead Attachment

Stitching With Beads

Small seed beads can be added to any cross-stitch design, using one bead per stitch. Knot thread at beginning of beaded section for security, especially if you are adding beads to clothing. The bead should lie in the same direction as the top half of cross-stitches.

Bead Attachment

Use one strand of floss to secure beads. Bring beading needle up from back of work (Fig. 8), leaving a 2-inch length of thread hanging; do not knot (end will be secured between stitches as you work). Thread bead on needle; complete stitch. Do not skip over more than two stitches or spaces without first securing thread, or last bead will be loose. To secure, weave thread into several stitches on back of work. Follow graph to work design, using one bead per stitch.

Planning a Project

Before you stitch, decide how large to cut fabric. Determine the stitched size and then allow enough additional fabric around the design plus 4 inches more on each side for use in finishing and mounting.

Cut your fabric exactly true, right along the holes of the fabric. Some raveling may occur as you handle the fabric. To minimize raveling along the raw edges, use an overcast basting stitch, machine zigzag-stitch or masking tape, which you can cut away when you are finished.

Finishing Needlework

When you have finished stitching, dampen your embroidery (or, if soiled, wash in lukewarm mild soapsuds and rinse well). Roll in a towel to remove excess moisture. Place facedown on a dry towel or padded surface; press carefully until dry and smooth. Make sure all thread ends are well anchored and clipped closely. Proceed with desired finishing.

Annie's®

Cross-Stitch Treasures for Children is published by Annie's, 306 East Parr Road, Berne, IN 46711. Printed in USA. Copyright © 2012, 2013 Annie's. All rights reserved. This publication may not be reproduced in part or in whole without written permission from the publisher.

RETAIL STORES: If you would like to carry this publication or any other Annie's publications, visit AnniesWSL.com.

Every effort has been made to ensure that the instructions in this pattern book are complete and accurate. We cannot, however, take responsibility for human error, typographical mistakes or variations in individual work. Please visit AnniesCustomerCare.com to check for pattern updates.

STAFF

Editor: Barb Sprunger
Technical Editor: Marla Laux
Copy Supervisor: Deborah Morgan
Copy Editors: Emily Carter, Samantha Schneider
Production Artist Supervisor: Erin Brandt
Graphic Artist: Amanda Treharn

Creative Director: Brad Snow
Assistant Art Director: Nick Pierce
Photography Supervisor: Tammy Christian
Photography: Matthew Owen
Photo Stylists: Tammy Liechty, Tammy Steiner

ISBN: 978-1-59635-617-7

2 3 4 5 6 7 8 9